JAPAN

Some things always stay the same in Japan. In the countryside, farmers grow rice, like the farmers of hundreds of years ago. Year after year, people stop to see the beautiful blossom on the cherry trees. In a small wooden house, tea is made, and visitors watch carefully.

But some things change very quickly. Better robots and newer phones! More exciting computer games! Taller buildings and faster trains! This is Japan – the old and the new together, always changing, and always the same.

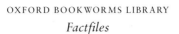

OXFORD BOOKWORMS LIBRARY
Factfiles

Japan

Stage 1 (400 headwords)

Factfiles Series Editor: Christine Lindop

RACHEL BLADON

Japan

OXFORD UNIVERSITY PRESS

OXFORD
UNIVERSITY PRESS

Great Clarendon Street, Oxford, OX2 6DP, United Kingdom

Oxford University Press is a department of the University of Oxford.
It furthers the University's objective of excellence in research, scholarship,
and education by publishing worldwide. Oxford is a registered trade
mark of Oxford University Press in the UK and in certain other countries

ISBN: 978 0 19 423669 0

A complete recording of *Japan* is available on CD. Pack ISBN: 978 0 19 423661 4

Printed in China

Word count (main text): 5,354

For more information on the Oxford Bookworms Library,
visit www.oup.com/elt/gradedreaders

ACKNOWLEDGEMENTS

Cover image: Corbis (Mount Fuji, Japan/David Ball)

Map by: Peter Bull p.2

The Publishers would like to thank the following for their permission to reproduce photographs:
Action Images Ltd p.21 (Yomiuri Giants Lee Seung-youp/); Alamy Images pp.13 (Traditional
Japanese house/Misha Gordon), 22 (Sumo wrestlers/Nic Cleave Photography), 25 (*Princess
Mononoké*/Photos 12), 37 (Bento box/Japanese Foods), 37 (Japanese restaurant/Salvo Severino),
40 (2012 Mitsubishi i MiEV electric car and a charging station/Oleksiy Maksymenko
Photography); Corbis pp.0 (Ornate Toshogu Shrine/Jeremy Woodhouse/Spaces Images),
1 (Women in kimonos/Haruyoshi Yamaguchi), 5 (Samurai warriors/Kimimasa Mayama/
epa), 8 (Sony LCD televisions/EPA/Kimimasa Mayama), 10 (Mt Fuji in Winter/Dex Image),
12 (Shinkansen/Jon Hicks), 14 (Japanese family meal/Datacraft Co., Ltd.), 15 (Women reading
newspaper/Franck Robichon/epa), 19 (Picnicking under cherry blossom/Michael S. Yamashita),
20 (Geisha/Peter Adams), 23 (Bunraku performance/Michael S. Yamashita), 24 (Under the Wave
off Kanagawa by Hokusai), 27 (Tokyo's City Hall building/Jose Fusta Raga), 29 (Senso-Ji Temple,
Asakusa/Jose Fuste Raga), 29 (Shibuya, Tokyo/Joachim Ladefoged/VII), 30 (Golden Pavilion/Keith
Levit/Design Pics), 31 (Peace Memorial Park, Hiroshima/Kimimasa Mayama/epa), 34 (Tempura
soba/Studio Eye), 36 (Table d'Hote/Studio Eye), 38 (Rice harvest/B.S.p.I.), 44 (Bathroom/Treve
Johnson/Lived In Images), cover (Mount Fuji - Japan/David Ball); Getty Images pp.7 (Hiroshima
ruins/Bernard Hoffman/Time Life Pictures), 9 (Japan tsunami devastation/Philippe Lopez/AFP),
11 (Spa/Tohoku Color Agency), 16 (Tea ceremony/DAJ), 18 (Kanda Matsuri/Kazuhiro Nogi/AFP),
26 (Shinjuku at night/Tom Bonaventure), 32 (Aharen Beach at Tokashiki Island/Melissa Tse),
33 (Snow sculpture, Sapporo/Glowimages), 35 (Sushi restaurant/Grant Faint), 39 (Nissan car
assembly/Junko Kimura); Mary Evans Picture Library p.6 (Tokugawa Ieyasu Japanese Shogun/
engraving by unknown artist); Oxford University Press pp.44 (Chopsticks and bowl of rice/
GLOW ASIA), 44 (Football/Score by Aflo), 44 (Winter near Mount Fuji/Image Plan), 44 (Fish on
barbecue/Image Source), 44 (Green hills/Imagemore).

CONTENTS

1   Old meets new

What do people know about Japan? Japan is in East Asia, in the Pacific Ocean – most people know that. Many people like *sushi*, and that comes from Japan. And everyone knows about Japanese *sumo* wrestling. But there are a lot more amazing things about this country.

Japan is one of the most exciting countries in the world. It is also a country with many different faces. In Japan, east meets west, and old meets new. Here you can find beautiful old wooden houses and big tall modern buildings in one street. You can visit ancient temples and shrines, and buy the newest computer games. Japan has some of the biggest cities in the world, and some of the most beautiful countryside.

Old meets new

Japan is a country of islands. It has four big islands – Honshu, Hokkaido, Kyushu, and Shikoku – and nearly seven thousand smaller ones. The country has many mountains, and there is not a lot of good land for buildings. Most Japanese people live in the big cities in the south and west of Honshu, away from the mountains. There are 128 million people in Japan, and nearly 69 million of them live near the Pacific Ocean between Osaka and the capital city, Tokyo.

You can find very different weather in the different islands of Japan. In the island of Hokkaido, the winters are long and cold, and the summers are warm. But in Okinawa and the Ryukyu islands in the south, it is warm in the winter and hot in the summer. So in December in Japan, you can go in the sea in the south, and go skiing in the mountains in the north!

Millions of people visit Japan every year. Japanese people like to help these visitors, and they are very polite to them. This is a very important thing for most Japanese people; they want to be polite to everyone.

Work and the family are also very important in Japan. Most Japanese people have two religions – Shintoism and Buddhism. People go to temples and shrines, and there are also many Shinto and Buddhist festivals in the year.

Some of Japan's industries make a lot of money. Japan makes about 10 million cars every year, and its electronics industry – cameras, computers, phones, and televisions – is famous around the world. Japan is always changing: it often makes or does new things first, and countries in the west often change things to be like Japan. But Japan does not forget its past. In the countryside, many Japanese work as farmers. They grow rice and catch fish, like people hundreds of years ago.

Many people come to Japan for business. But many also come to see the country's beautiful art, temples, and gardens. They go to the theatre, and eat well in Japan's many wonderful restaurants. Japan has something for everyone – its cities are new and exciting, but this amazing country has ancient buildings and culture too.

2 Emperors, samurai, and shoguns

Many of the important things about life in Japan today were also important more than 1,500 years ago. Japan is near to Korea and China, and many ideas came to ancient Japan from people in these countries. Like Korean and Chinese people, the ancient Japanese learned to grow rice and to make cloth. Buddhism came to Japan from Korea and China, and by the 400s, the Japanese began to use Chinese *kanji*, or picture-words, for writing.

From the 600s, emperors ruled Japan. Families came together into groups called clans around these important rulers. The clans fought for power all the time.

In 794, the Japanese emperor moved his home to Kyoto. This was a quiet time in Japan, and art and writing became very important. In the early 1000s in Kyoto, a woman called Murasaki Shikibu wrote *The Tale of Genji*, and people read this interesting book even now.

At this time, fighters became very powerful in Japan. At first they worked for important men in different parts of the country. When the fighters were there, the land and homes of these men were safe. But the very best fighters now made new clans, called *samurai*. The samurai were very powerful. The most powerful of the samurai were called *shoguns*, and these shoguns wanted to rule Japan.

A samurai

Tokugawa Ieyasu

In 1185, the emperor lost power, and Minamoto no Yoritomo became the first shogun ruler of Japan. For the next seven hundred years, different shoguns ruled Japan, and again and again the clans fought.

In 1600, the shoguns of the Tokugawa clan came to power. The first of these, Tokugawa Ieyasu, made his home at Edo (now Tokyo). Now they were in power, the Tokugawa shoguns wanted to stay there. They made a class system: they gave everyone a place, from the shoguns and samurai at the top down to farmers and workers.

Under the Tokugawa, Edo became bigger and more important, and there was a lot of art and theatre. But in 1639, the Tokugawa closed Japan to the world. For two hundred years, people from other countries could not come in and out of Japan, and Japanese people could not leave.

This stopped in 1853, when American ships came to Japan. They wanted to buy Japanese goods, and to bring American goods into Japan. The Tokugawa shoguns now lost their power, and from 1868 the emperors again ruled Japan.

After this, Japan began to change. The emperor broke down the class system of the Tokugawa shoguns. School became a part of life for all Japanese children. Japan began to make things and sell them to other countries, and people came to Japan to do business. Toyoda Sakichi was a very important person in Japan at this time. First he changed things in the cloth industry, and after that people could work better and faster. Later his business began to make cars too, and the Toyota Motor Corporation was born.

Japan fought in the First World War (1914–18), and by the 1920s it was an important country in the world. In the Second World War (1939–45) Japan fought in the Pacific. In August 1945, US atomic bombs killed more than 200,000 Japanese in the cities of Hiroshima and Nagasaki.

Hiroshima after the bomb

Bombs destroyed many of Japan's cities and industries in the war. But because Japanese people worked hard and had good ideas, Japan's industries began to grow. At first, Japan made cars, ships, and steel, but in the 1970s, the electronics industry became more important. Japan began to make phones, televisions, computers, and cameras. Soon Japan was famous around the world for its new ideas in the electronics industry.

Then, from the 1990s, industries in other countries in Asia began to grow, and there were hard times for Japan. But Japan is the country of Canon, Toyota, Mitsubishi, and Sony, and we see names like these every day on things in our homes, schools, and places of work.

3 Earthquakes and volcanoes

On 11 March 2011, there was a big earthquake east of the city of Sendai in the northeast of Japan. Then a tsunami, 40 metres high, came onto the land and destroyed everything in front of it. More than 18,000 people died, and many more lost their homes.

This was not Japan's first big earthquake. In 1995, the Great Hanshin earthquake killed more than 6,000 people in and near the city of Kobe, and destroyed more than 100,000 buildings. And in 1923, the Great Kanto Earthquake destroyed a lot of Tokyo. But new buildings and roads in Japan are better now. They move a lot in

After the tsunami

an earthquake, so the earthquake does not destroy them. Because of this, in March 2011, many buildings stayed standing in the earthquake – but the tsunami brought them down.

There are about 1,500 earthquakes a year in Japan, but most of them are small. So why does Japan have so many earthquakes? In this part of the world, under the Pacific Ocean, the land is always moving. Because of this, there are often earthquakes, and many of Japan's mountains are volcanoes. About fifteen times a year, people near a volcano in different parts of Japan see smoke and hear noise from the mountain.

The most famous volcano is Mount Fuji, the highest mountain in the country at 3,776 metres. Mount Fuji is very beautiful, and many people visit it.

Mount Fuji

A hot spring

Because of Japan's many volcanoes, it also has more than two thousand hot springs. Many people come to the springs, to keep well or just because they like the warm water.

People in Japan must be careful about volcanoes and earthquakes, but sometimes they must keep safe in typhoons too. Typhoons come from the Pacific; they bring very bad weather with powerful winds. They usually come to Japan between July and October. Typhoons destroy buildings and roads. Hills sometimes break away in the rain, and often people die.

When there is a big typhoon or an earthquake, Japanese people move quickly. In a typhoon, they stay in their buildings and move away from windows. In an earthquake, they move under a table and stay safe there.

4 Life in Japan

Most Japanese people live in cities. But others live in the suburbs – places near a big city – and go to and from work every day. Their working day is usually very long, and often they live far away from their work. There are many, many people and cars in Japanese cities, and sometimes there is bad air pollution.

There are lots of buses and trains in Japan, and they are usually very good. Trains carry thousands of people under the big cities. Other trains, called *shinkansen*, go across the country. Shinkansen are some of the best trains in the world; they can go at 300 kilometres per hour, and they are nearly always on time.

Shinkansen in Tokyo

In a Japanese home

What are Japanese homes like? Old Japanese houses were wooden, and had paper doors. On the floors, they had mats called *tatami*. They had Japanese beds called *futons*. People usually put these away in the day, because their homes were not very big.

Most new houses in Japan are wooden, but many people live in apartments in big buildings. They often have beds, not futons, because their homes are bigger, but many still have some tatami mats.

In Japanese homes there are often Buddhist or Shinto altars, and families come to these small places to pray. There are many Buddhist temples in Japan, and also thousands of Shinto shrines. People go there to pray at festivals and at important times, for example when a child is born.

Like their families, children work very hard. Children must go to school from six years old, but many children begin school at only three or four. Children go to

Most families eat together

elementary school for six years, and then they move to junior high school and high school. Many children go to classes in things like English and music after their day at school. Children can leave school when they are fifteen, but more than 90 per cent of children stay at school. After that, many young Japanese people become students for some years.

Then they need to find work. In the cities, many people work in business, and for the big industries – steel, ships, cars, and electronics. In the countryside, people often live on small family farms, growing things like rice, tea, and apples. Fishing is an important industry in Japan too. People get fish from the sea or have fish farms.

Japanese people work very hard, but family life is very important to them too. Most Japanese families eat together at home, and some people go to live with their son's or daughter's family when they get old. Old people are very important in Japan, and people are usually polite to them. At weekends, families often go out together, or watch television or play computer games at home.

5   Language and customs

Most people can learn a little Japanese, and Japanese people like it when visitors speak their language. But to speak Japanese well – that is not easy!

There are three kinds of writing in Japanese. In *kanji*, pictures make words, but in *hiragana* and *katakana* there is a 'letter' for every sound. You use hiragana for Japanese words, and katakana for words from other languages, like English.

At a tea ceremony

You can learn hiragana and katakana quickly, and say the words easily. But that is not everything! In Japanese, you use different words for older and younger people, and for important people. Men and women use different words too. And people speak Japanese differently in different parts of the country. So you need to learn a lot of different things!

There are other things to learn about life in Japan. For example, never wash in the bath in Japan. Japanese people always wash *outside* the bath first, so the dirty water stays out of the bath. *Then* they get into the bath.

You must be careful about shoes in Japan too. Japanese people do not wear their shoes in the house. They leave their shoes at the door, so the floor or the tatami mats do not get dirty. Sometimes Japanese people wear wooden shoes called *geta*. You can get these shoes on and off easily when you need to.

Saying hello to people in Japan is different too. Japanese people bow when they meet people, and they give a bigger bow for older or more important people. When you talk to or about someone, you must always put -*san* or -*sama* after their name.

Japan has many old customs, and one of the most important is the tea ceremony. Tea came to Japan from China in the 700s. At a tea ceremony, everyone first meets the other people at the ceremony, and then walks in the garden of the tea-house. In a small room, the tea-maker then makes green tea, very carefully, and everyone watches. Now the visitors bow, drink their tea, and eat. At a tea ceremony, everyone must 'live now'. You must watch the tea and the tea-maker, and not think about other things!

Many visitors like to go to a tea ceremony, and many also like to see Japan's famous cherry blossom. There are many cherry trees in Japan, and in April they always have lots of beautiful blossom. At this time, lots of people go out to sit and eat under the trees (in the day and at night) and look at the blossom. There are cherry blossom festivals too.

These cherry blossom festivals are some of many festivals in Japan at different times in the year. Festivals are very important for Japanese people. The most important festival is New Year's Day, when families often

The *Kanda Matsuri* festival

Under the cherry trees

visit temples and shrines. Many people eat noodles on the day before New Year's Day, because they want to live for a long time. Does this help? Well – perhaps!

In November, for one of these festivals, families take three-, five- and seven-year-old children to shrines, and you can see many children in beautiful clothes. At the shrines, families say thank you for their children, and pray for them.

One of the biggest and most famous festivals in Tokyo is the *Kanda Matsuri* in May. For this festival, people wear clothes from old times, and carry a hundred small shrines through the streets of Tokyo. Japanese people and visitors love watching this very happy festival.

For festivals, and for other important days, many people in Japan wear wonderful clothes called *kimonos*.

A geisha in a red kimono

New kimonos are very expensive, but beautiful, and people often keep them in their families for many years. Women wear kimonos, carry fans, and wear beautiful combs in their hair.

Some women, called *geisha*, wear kimonos to work! The first geisha began to work in Japan about three hundred years ago, and you can find them in some cities today. Geisha learn Japanese arts like music and singing. They wear wonderful kimonos, and do their hair with beautiful combs. Their faces are very white, and their mouths are red.

6   Sport and culture

What other things do Japanese people like to do at the weekends? Sport is very important in Japan, of course. Many Japanese like to watch and play baseball, and thousands of people go to see famous teams like the Yomiuri Giants and the Yakult Swallows. Many Japanese began to play football after the 2002 FIFA World Cup in Japan and Korea, and in 2011, the Japanese Women's Football Team came home from Germany with the World Cup! Sawa Homare, the best player in the team, was the 2011 FIFA Best Player of the Year.

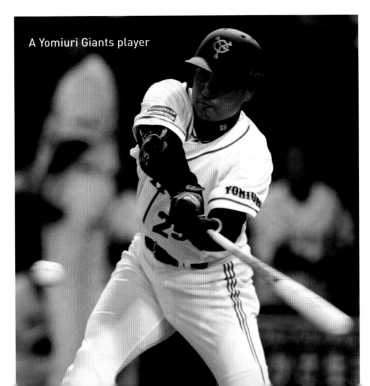

A Yomiuri Giants player

Sumo wrestling

Many people in Japan like to watch sumo wrestling. It began in Japan nearly two thousand years ago. In wrestling, two men fight in a ring. They wear only a kind of cloth called a *mawashi*, and they wear their hair like an ancient samurai. One wrestler must get the other out of the ring, or down to the floor. The best wrestlers are very famous in Japan, but they work very hard. Young wrestlers go into a *heya*, or wrestling club, when they are only about fifteen years old. There they must work for the older wrestlers, and learn to fight, and they do not usually go home or see their families for years.

Many Japanese children learn sports like *judo* and *kendo* in schools and clubs, and skiing, mountain walking, and running are also important sports in Japan.

Many people in Japan like to go to the theatre in the evenings or at weekends. There are different kinds of Japanese theatre. *Noh* theatre is the oldest kind. There are no women, and usually there are only one or two men, and there is music and singing. In *Kabuki* theatre you see a lot of men, with amazing clothes in many colours.

Bunraku is a kind of puppet theatre. The puppets are often 1 metre high or more, and three people in black clothes work together to move each puppet. Chikamatsu Monzaemon is one of Japan's most famous writers for theatre. He wrote about a hundred stories for the bunraku theatre, and you can see many in Japan today.

Bunraku theatre

Many kinds of music are important in Japanese culture. One interesting kind of music from old times is *gagaku*. You can hear gagaku today at some Shinto shrines and Buddhist temples. And of course many Japanese people like pop music too.

Art and crafts are important in Japanese life. Some of these first came to Japan in ancient times: calligraphy (a kind of beautiful writing), *ikebana* (working with flowers), and *bonsai* (small and beautiful trees). In the early 1800s, people began to make and sell *ukiyo-e* – pictures of geisha, the theatre, or beautiful things like cherry blossom. One of the most famous names from this time is Hokusai. He made pictures of the countryside of Japan, and *The Great Wave*, one of his pictures from the 1830s, is famous around the world.

Japan is now known for its modern art too, and in many of its crafts people can see the arts of old Japan with new ideas from the west.

The Great Wave, by Hokusai

From the anime film
Princess Mononoke

There is art in everything in Japan. Japanese food is not only very good to eat – it is also beautiful to look at. Japanese gardens, too, are works of art. They change a lot at different times of the year.

What about modern culture in Japan? *Karaoke* is important, of course, and many people go out to sing karaoke with friends, or do karaoke at home.

Manga and *anime* are also a very big part of modern Japanese culture. In manga, pictures tell a story in a book; in anime, pictures tell a story in a film. Young and old people read manga – there are manga for everything from baseball to love stories! You can buy manga at many shops, and Japan now has manga cafes. In these places you can have a drink, read manga, and watch TV or anime. Millions of people like anime too. Films like *Akira* and *Spirited Away* are famous in Japan and in many other countries.

7 Tokyo

Most visitors to Japan go to Tokyo, of course. Tokyo is the capital – the most important city – of Japan, and it is an amazing place. More than thirty-five million people live here, but it is very safe, and you can get around easily by bus or train.

People and cars make lots of noise in Tokyo. But here you can also find quiet places – ancient temples, beautiful gardens, and old wooden houses.

One of the most interesting parts of Tokyo is Shinjuku. Here there are big department stores – modern shops with many different kinds of goods. There are amazing buildings hundreds of metres high, restaurants, cinemas, art galleries, and one of Tokyo's biggest gardens too. Shinjuku has something of everything!

Shinjuku

The TMGB

People go to West Shinjuku to work, and they go to East Shinjuku to play! More than 250,000 people work in the tall buildings of West Shinjuku. One of these is the famous Tokyo Metropolitan Government Building (TMGB), by Kenzo Tange. Tange was famous for many wonderful buildings in Japan and around the world. Many of his buildings, like the TMGB, feel old and Japanese but new and exciting too.

In East Shinjuku, you can eat, shop, and go to the cinema. You can also walk in the beautiful gardens at Shinjuku Gyoen.

Near Shinjuku is Meiji-Jingu, the most important Shinto shrine in Tokyo. The shrine was made in the 1920s to remember Emperor Meiji and his wife, and there is a beautiful garden there. The emperor's wife loved to visit it and see the flowers. At New Year, more than three million people come to Meiji-Jingu to pray.

A very important place for the Buddhist religion in Tokyo is the famous Senso-ji temple at Asakusa. There are always a lot of people at the temple, and you can feel the amazing past of this ancient place.

The Imperial Palace is very old too. The Emperor and his family live in the palace now, but in 1593, Tokugawa Ieyasu, the first of the Tokugawa shoguns, began to make a castle here. It soon became the world's biggest castle. On 23 December and 2 January, the gardens nearest to the palace are open, and thousands of people go to see the Emperor and his family. On other days, you can walk in the beautiful East Gardens.

There are beautiful gardens in Ueno Park, too – and here you can also see temples, shrines, and the famous Tokyo National Museum. The museum has some amazing Japanese art, and also ancient things from Japan and other places in Asia.

Many people go to Shibuya and Ginza for their shops. In Ginza, you can find big department stores, and also very small craft shops. Some people wear their best clothes in Ginza, because it is a very expensive part of Tokyo. Go to

Senso-ji temple

Shibuya at night

the Matsuya department store and look at the beautiful kimonos there. Or go into the Sony building. There you can see the newest cameras, phones, and electronics.

In Shibuya, modern Tokyo hits you in the face! Here you can shop for the newest clothes and music, and in the evening, Tokyo's young people come to the many restaurants and clubs.

You can visit many other places in Tokyo. Go to Akihabara to buy cheap electronics or manga. Visit the Tsukiji Fish Market – people from restaurants and food shops come here and buy the best fish in Japan. Go up the new Tokyo Sky Tree, the tallest building in Japan at 634 metres. Visit the art galleries at Roppongi, or more of Tokyo's many museums. And, of course, have wonderful food. There is something for every visitor in this amazing city!

8 Other places to visit

For many people, Kyoto is one of the most important cities to visit in Japan. Kyoto was the capital of Japan for more than a thousand years. Today, Kyoto has big department stores with everything for modern life in Japan. But it is an ancient city too, with mountains around it. And on the many walks around Kyoto you can see old wooden houses, beautiful temples and palaces, and wonderful gardens.

Kinkaju-ji temple

The A-Bomb Dome, Hiroshima

In Kyoto, visit the beautiful Kinkaku-ji temple on the lake. Walk around Higashiyama too. Here you can see the famous Kiyomizu temple, and many other temples, gardens and museums. In Gion, people in wonderful geisha clothes walk in the streets. Some of the most important people in Japan come to Gion to eat in the restaurants or visit the old wooden tea-houses.

An important visit for many people is to the Peace Memorial Park and Museum at Hiroshima. Here you can learn about the atomic bombs of 1945, and see the A-bomb Dome. This is one of the only buildings in Hiroshima from the time of the atomic bomb.

Between Tokyo and Hiroshima is Osaka, one of Japan's biggest cities after Tokyo. Osaka is famous for its food, and also for its night life. Here you can find music and theatre, but also art galleries and some amazing new buildings. The Umeda Sky Building is 173 metres high, and the Floating Garden Observatory goes between two parts of it. You can see all of Osaka from there!

From Osaka it is not far to Himeji-jo, the best of Japan's old castles. The castle became famous at the time of the Tokugawa shoguns, and is a true samurai castle. And Nara is also near Osaka. Nara was the old capital of Japan before Kyoto, and it has many Buddhist temples. Here, in the hills, is Todai-ji temple, the biggest wooden building in the world.

But Japan is not just a place of exciting cities and ancient culture. You can get away from it all in Okinawa, in the far south of Japan. Here it is warm all year. There are 160 islands in Okinawa, and in the beautiful water of the Pacific you can see amazing fish and sea animals. Okinawa is also famous for its old castles, friendly people, good food, and beautiful crafts.

Okinawa

Do you like walking in the mountains and the countryside? Then you must visit Hokkaido, the big island in the north of Japan. The countryside here is beautiful, and there are many wonderful animals and flowers. In the winter, you can go skiing in Hokkaido, and in the capital, Sapporo, there is a Snow Festival every year.

The Snow Festival, Sapporo

From Tokyo it is not far to Hakone, a beautiful town with lakes, mountains, and hot springs. Here you can see beautiful Mount Fuji, look at some wonderful art in the Pola Museum, or visit Lake Ashinoko. Hakone is next to an old volcano; you can smell the hot air, and there are lots of hot springs. In the summer, in July and August, many people go up Mount Fuji. They take the bus first, and then walk for five or six hours to the top of the mountain. It is a hard walk, but it is beautiful at the top!

9   Japanese food

Tempura

One of the most wonderful things about a visit to Japan is the amazing food. There are many restaurants in Japan, and every town or place has different kinds of food. Different times of year bring new foods to the table too. Japanese food is always good, and it often looks beautiful. Japanese people make their food very carefully.

There are many different kinds of restaurant in Japan. You can eat at a cheap noodle shop, or have a drink with some food at an *izakaya*. Many restaurants are not very expensive, and you can look at the food in the windows before you eat. But for the very best food, in a beautiful place, people go to *ryotei*. These restaurants have gardens, and beautiful rooms – but sometimes only people known to the *ryotei* can get tables.

Many Japanese restaurants have just one important kind of food – for example, there are restaurants for *tempura* (fish and vegetables in batter). In *kaiten-zushi* shops there is *sashimi* (fish) and *sushi* (cold rice with fish or vegetables) on a moving table. When you see something nice, you take it!

A *kaiten-zushi* shop

Fish, vegetables, and noodles are all very important in Japanese food, but rice is the most important thing. There is always *miso* soup too. Often there is just a little of everything, but it all looks beautiful. People eat rice, miso soup, and fish or vegetables for breakfast!

People at work, at school, or going on a train do not usually take sandwiches – they take a *bento* box. A bento box has different kinds of food – always with rice – in a box, and you can find these in many shops.

Green tea is an important drink in Japan. Most people like to drink coffee too, and there are lots of coffee shops in Japan. Then there is *sake*. This is made from rice, and you can drink it warm in winter. People drink beer too, and you can get very good Japanese whisky.

A *bento* box

In a Japanese restaurant

In many Japanese restaurants, you sit on the floor, on tatami mats. Before you eat, the people in the restaurant give you a hot or cold cloth for your hands. Then the food arrives. You eat Japanese food with wooden sticks called chopsticks.

Here are some things to remember. Do not stand your chopsticks in your rice – this is not polite in Japan. Do not eat some things but leave others – eat all your food. Before you eat, say '*Itadakimasu,*' and when you finish, you can say, '*Gochiso-sama deshita!*' (That was very good!) In Japan, that is nearly always true.

10   Into the future

Some things in Japan are changing all the time, and others are no different from hundreds of years ago! So what is Japan's future?

One big change coming for Japan is in its people. The number of people in Japan is getting smaller, because people are having smaller families. Women are working for longer and having children later, so their families are smaller.

There are also many more old people in Japan today. More than 20 per cent of Japanese people are older than 65, because people now live much longer. In the past in Japan, women always helped the old people in their family, but many more women work now. So who is going to help these old people, and where is the money going to come

Old people at work

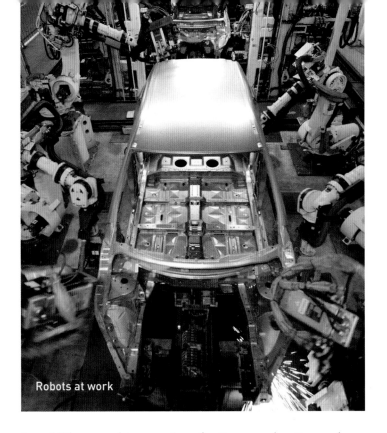
Robots at work

from? These are big questions for Japan today. But perhaps the old people have the answer. Because they eat well and have good doctors and hospitals, old Japanese people often stay well for a very long time. So perhaps working longer, into their 70s or 80s, is the future for old people.

Japan's industries are changing, too. In the 1990s, countries like China and Korea began to make electronic goods very cheaply. Many countries got their electronic goods from these countries, not from Japan. So now, Japan does not make many of these goods. Japan makes more 'one of a kind' goods, for example, the very best cameras, and amazing computer games. Japan also has half of the world's robots. Robots are becoming more and more important in the modern world, and again, Japan is in front here.

An electric car

With more and more cars in Japan, many cities have bad air pollution. Japan is working with other countries around the world to fight air pollution. Japan's car industry is working hard on this; some of their new small cars use electricity, and Japanese people are thinking of other ideas for the future.

There is also the question of nuclear power. Before 2011, about 25 per cent of Japan's electricity came from nuclear power. Japan wanted to have more nuclear power stations. But the earthquake and tsunami of 2011 destroyed part of a nuclear power station near Sendai, so it was not safe. More than 80,000 people had to leave their homes. Now many people are afraid of nuclear power. So how is Japan going to make its electricity in the future? Like many other countries, Japan is now looking at things like the sun and the wind to do this.

Japan of course has many exciting new ideas. The people of this amazing country, with their wonderful ancient culture, are so often the first to take the world into the future.

GLOSSARY

air pollution   when air is made dirty and dangerous by gases
from cars, factories, etc
amazing   very interesting and different
ancient   very old
around   in different places; on all sides of something
art   pictures and other beautiful things that people like to look
at; **art gallery** a place where you can see paintings and other
kinds of art
atomic bomb   a very powerful bomb that uses the energy from
splitting an atom
bath   a long container that you sit in to wash your body
become (past tense **became**)   to grow or change and begin to be
something
bow   to bend your head or body forward to show respect
bus   a kind of big 'car' which many people can travel in
business   buying and selling things; a place where people sell or
make things
buy   to give money for something
castle   a large old building where an important person could live
safely
city   a big and important town
cloth   material made of wool, cotton, etc, that you use for
making clothes and other things
clothes   things you wear, e.g. shirts, trousers, dresses
club   a place where you go to dance and listen to music; a place
where people meet to do the same thing together
computer game   a game played on a computer
countryside   land that is away from towns, with trees, rivers, etc
craft   making beautiful things with your hands
destroy   when something is destroyed, it is dead and finished (e.g.
fire destroys a forest)
earthquake   a sudden strong shaking of the ground

electricity power that comes through wires and makes machines work

electronic things like TVs and computers that have a lot of very small parts and use electricity

emperor a very powerful man who rules a country

fan something you hold in your hand and move to make the air cooler

farm a place where people keep animals and grow food

festival a time when a lot of people come together to have fun, make music, dance, etc

fight to try to hurt or kill somebody

fish an animal that lives in water; the food from that animal; **fishing** catching fish as a business

floor the part of a room that you walk on

food what you eat

goods things that you buy or sell

grow to get bigger; to put a plant in the ground and look after it

hard difficult; **work hard** to work with a lot of effort

idea a plan or new thought

industry all the companies in a country that make the same thing

island a piece of land with water around it

kind a group of things that are the same in some way

land the part of the earth that is not the sea; a piece of ground

life the way that you live

modern of the present time

mountain a very high hill

museum a place where you can look at old or interesting things

music when you sing or play an instrument, you make music

nuclear power electricity made from splitting atoms; **nuclear power station** a building where this kind of electricity is made

other different

part one of the pieces of something

place where something or somebody is

polite   speaking or behaving in a way that shows respect

power   the ability to control people or things; (*adj*) **powerful**

pray   to speak to a god

restaurant   a place where people can buy and eat meals

rule   to control a country; (*n*) **ruler**

safe   not in danger

shogun   a powerful ruler from a clan of samurai fighters

skiing   a sport where you move across the snow on long flat
   pieces of wood

sport   a game like football, tennis, etc

steel   very strong metal that is used for making things like knives,
   parts of buildings, etc

story   words that tell you about what happened in a certain place
   or time

tea   a hot drink made with the leaves of a special plant;
   tea-house a special building where tea is made

team   a group of people who play a sport together against
   another group

temple   a building where people go to say prayers to gods

theatre   a building where you go to see plays; stories performed
   by actors

together   with another person

tsunami   a very big wall of water from the sea after an
   earthquake

use   to do a job with something

volcano   a mountain with a hole in the top where fire sometimes
   comes out

war   fighting between countries or groups of people

wash   to make yourself clean with water

wooden   made of wood from a tree

world   the earth with all its countries and people

ACTIVITIES

Before Reading

1 Match the words to the pictures. You can use a dictionary.

1 ☐ fish   3 ☐ football   5 ☐ rice
2 ☐ bath   4 ☐ mountain   6 ☐ countryside

2 How much do you know about Japan? Three of these sentences are true – which ones are they?

1 There are three festivals in Japan every year.
2 Japanese people eat rice for breakfast.
3 In Japan, people never wash in the bath.
4 Japanese people do not like baseball.
5 Japan has nearly 7,000 islands.
6 Most Japanese people live in the countryside.

ACTIVITIES

While Reading

Read Chapter 1, then match these halves of sentences.

1 Japan has . . .
2 In Hokkaido and the islands in the north, . . .
3 In the south of Japan, . . .
4 Japan makes about . . .
5 In the countryside, many Japanese . . .
6 Japan has new, exciting cities, . . .

a 10 million cars every year.

b the winters are long and cold.

c work as farmers.

d and ancient buildings and culture too.

e you can go in the sea in December.

f some of the biggest cities in the world.

Read Chapter 2, then put these sentences in the right order.

1 US atomic bombs killed people in Hiroshima and Nagasaki.
2 The Tokugawa shoguns closed Japan to the world.
3 Buddhism came to Japan from Korea and China.
4 The electronics industry became important in Japan.
5 Minamoto no Yoritomo became the first shogun ruler of Japan.
6 The Tokugawa shoguns lost their power.
7 Japan fought in the First World War.
8 The shoguns of the Tokugawa clan came to power.

Read Chapters 3 and 4, then complete these sentences with the correct numbers.

6, 15, 90, 300, 1,500, 2,000, 3,776, 18,000

1 More than _____ people died in the 2011 earthquake and tsunami.

2 There are about _____ earthquakes a year in Japan.

3 Mount Fuji is _____ metres high.

4 Japan has more than _____ hot springs.

5 Shinkansen can go at _____ kilometres per hour.

6 Japanese children must go to school from _____ years old.

7 Japanese children can leave school when they are _____.

8 More than _____ per cent of children stay at school after they are fifteen.

Read Chapter 5, then rewrite these untrue sentences with the correct information.

1 There are two kinds of writing in Japanese.

2 Japanese people always have a bath first, and then wash.

3 Japanese people always wear their shoes in the house.

4 When you talk to or about someone, you must always put *-san* or *-sama* before their name.

5 Tea came to Japan from Korea in the 700s.

6 Japan's cherry trees always have lots of beautiful blossom in December.

7 Many people eat apples on the day before New Year's Day, because they want to live for a long time.

8 The Kanda Matsuri is one of the biggest and most famous festivals in Kyoto.

9 Geisha wear beautiful clothes called geta.

Read Chapter 6. Match the words with their meanings.

1 heya	a	picture-story books
2 bunraku	b	Japanese music from old times
3 gagaku	c	a sumo wrestling club
4 ikebana	d	picture-story films
5 bonsai	e	Japanese pictures from old times
6 ukiyo-e	f	the art of working with flowers
7 manga	g	a kind of puppet theatre
8 anime	h	small and beautiful trees

Read Chapter 7. Choose the best question-words for these questions, and then answer them.

How / How many / What / When / Which / Where / Who / Why

1 . . . people live in Tokyo?
2 . . . happens in West Shinjuku's tall buildings?
3 . . . can you do in East Shinjuku?
4 . . . was Meiji-Jingu shrine made?
5 . . . famous temple is at Asakusa?
6 . . . lives in the Imperial Palace?
7 . . . is the Tokyo National Museum?
8 . . . in Tokyo can you find big department stores and small craft shops?
9 . . . do people visit the Tsukiji Fish Market?
10 . . . tall is the Tokyo Sky Tree?

Read Chapter 8, then complete the sentences with the names of the places.

1 In _____, you can visit Kinkaku-ji temple.

2 Many people visit the Peace Memorial Park and Museum at _____.

3 From the Floating Garden Observatory on the Umeda Sky Building, you can see all of _____.

4 The best of Japan's old castles is _____.

5 At _____, you can see Todai-ji temple.

6 It is warm all year in the 160 islands of _____.

7 Sapporo is the capital of _____.

8 _____ is a beautiful town next to an old volcano.

Read Chapters 9 and 10, then circle *a*, *b*, or *c*.

1 For the very best food, people go to a _____.
   a) kaiten-zushi   b) izakaya   c) ryotei

2 The most important Japanese food is _____.
   a) rice   b) fish   c) noodles

3 People at work, at school, or going on a train often take _____.
   a) a bento box   b) sandwiches   c) miso soup

4 In Japan people eat food with _____.
   a) their hands   b) a cloth   c) wooden sticks

5 The number of people in Japan is getting smaller, because there are _____.
   a) not many old people   b) smaller families these days
   c) many earthquakes

6 _____ are not important in Japan's industries now.
   a) 'One of a kind' goods   b) Cheap electronic goods
   c) Robots

ACTIVITIES

After Reading

1 Find ten words from the book in this wordsearch and use them to complete the passage.

A	G	T	F	R	C	O	L	A	E	D
Y	A	O	C	L	O	T	H	E	S	A
R	L	V	Y	U	M	W	A	S	T	M
N	L	B	U	Y	P	Y	U	I	O	U
R	E	S	T	A	U	R	A	N	T	S
U	R	P	R	E	T	B	R	E	U	I
R	I	O	N	R	E	F	T	O	J	C
N	E	R	M	L	R	F	O	O	D	I
T	S	T	H	E	A	T	R	E	N	L

At the weekends, many Japanese like to watch and play _____, for example football, baseball, and sumo wrestling. Many people like to go to the _____ and watch noh, kabuki or bunraku. _____ is important in Japan too: people go to _____ where they can see amazing pictures by people like Hokusai.

There is _____ too, of course: people sing karaoke with their friends or go to pop concerts. Japan has many wonderful _____ with amazing _____, for example tempura, sashimi and sushi.

Many people go shopping too. They like to _____ the newest _____, music, and manga. But often people just like to stay at home and watch television or play _____ games.

2 **Here is an e-mail about a visit to Japan. Circle the correct words.**

Dear Mrs Wright

Here is some information about your visit to Japan next week:

Monday
Arrive in *Tokyo / Nara*, the capital city of Japan.

Tuesday
Morning: Visit Meiji-jingu, an important *Buddhist / Shinto* shrine.
Afternoon: Go shopping in *Shinjuku / Akihabara* (lots of big department stores)
Evening: Dinner at a kaiten-zushi shop (famous for *fish / noodles*!)

Wednesday
Morning: Visit *the Imperial Palace / Himeji-jo Castle*, home to the Emperor and his family.
Afternoon: Go up the *Tokyo Metropolitan Government Building / Tokyo Sky Tree*, the tallest building in Japan
Evening: Go by shinkansen (at *300 / 500* kilometres per hour!) to Kyoto.

Thursday
Morning: Visit the famous *Kiyomizu / Kinkaku-ji* temple on the lake.
Afternoon: Visit Gion. Here you can see people in wonderful geisha clothes with *red / white* faces.
Evening: One of Japan's most important old customs, *the tea ceremony / a karaoke evening*.

Friday
Morning: Go to Hiroshima to visit the *Peace Memorial Museum / Umeda Sky Building*.
Evening: Leave Japan from Kansai Airport near Osaka (famous for its *hot springs / nightlife*)

3 Now plan a five-day visit for a tourist to your country.
   Write an e-mail to them. Tell them what they are going to
   do on their trip.

4 What Japanese things can you find in your home, school or
   town? Make a list. Look for things like this:

   • cameras, TVs, phones, computers
   • cars
   • food and drinks
   • clothes
   • pictures
   • films and books
   • computer games

   Now compare your list with another student's. What things
   are the same? What things are different?

5 Would you like to live in Japan? Why / Why not? Would
   you like to visit Japan? What five things would you like to
   see and do in Japan? What would you like to see first?

6 Compare Japan and your country. You can use the
   information in this book. These websites can help you too:
   http://www.japan-guide.com/
   http://www.lonelyplanet.com/japan
   http://www.jnto.go.jp/eng/
   http://www.japantravelinfo.com

   You can begin like this:

   There are 128 million people in Japan, but in my country
   there are _____. In Japan, most people live in big cities.
   In my country, most people live _____.

ABOUT THE AUTHOR

Rachel Bladon has been a writer and editor of children's and educational books for many years. She has written for the Oxford Classic Tales and Read and Discover series, and has worked on other Bookworms Factfiles.

While living in Hong Kong and working as a commissioning editor for Asia, she visited and travelled in Japan several times, and greatly enjoyed exploring this beautiful country. This gave her a love of Japanese food and culture, and she subsequently studied Japanese and also did a Japanese cookery course. She and her family now live in Oxfordshire, England.

OXFORD BOOKWORMS LIBRARY

Classics • Crime & Mystery • Factfiles • Fantasy & Horror
Human Interest • Playscripts • Thriller & Adventure
True Stories • World Stories

The OXFORD BOOKWORMS LIBRARY provides enjoyable reading in English, with a wide range of classic and modern fiction, non-fiction, and plays. It includes original and adapted texts in seven carefully graded language stages, which take learners from beginner to advanced level. An overview is given on the next pages.

All Stage 1 titles are available as audio recordings, as well as over eighty other titles from Starter to Stage 6. All Starters and many titles at Stages 1 to 4 are specially recommended for younger learners. Every Bookworm is illustrated, and Starters and Factfiles have full-colour illustrations.

The OXFORD BOOKWORMS LIBRARY also offers extensive support. Each book contains an introduction to the story, notes about the author, a glossary, and activities. Additional resources include tests and worksheets, and answers for these and for the activities in the books. There is advice on running a class library, using audio recordings, and the many ways of using Oxford Bookworms in reading programmes. Resource materials are available on the website <www.oup.com/bookworms>.

The *Oxford Bookworms Collection* is a series for advanced learners. It consists of volumes of short stories by well-known authors, both classic and modern. Texts are not abridged or adapted in any way, but carefully selected to be accessible to the advanced student.

You can find details and a full list of titles in the *Oxford Bookworms Library Catalogue* and *Oxford English Language Teaching Catalogues*, and on the website <www.oup.com/bookworms>.

THE OXFORD BOOKWORMS LIBRARY GRADING AND SAMPLE EXTRACTS

STARTER • 250 HEADWORDS

present simple – present continuous – imperative –
can/cannot, must – going to (future) – simple gerunds …

Her phone is ringing – but where is it?

Sally gets out of bed and looks in her bag. No phone. She looks under the bed. No phone. Then she looks behind the door. There is her phone. Sally picks up her phone and answers it. *Sally's Phone*

STAGE 1 • 400 HEADWORDS

… past simple – coordination with and, but, or –
subordination with before, after, when, because, so …

I knew him in Persia. He was a famous builder and I worked with him there. For a time I was his friend, but not for long. When he came to Paris, I came after him – I wanted to watch him. He was a very clever, very dangerous man. *The Phantom of the Opera*

STAGE 2 • 700 HEADWORDS

… present perfect – will (future) – (don't) have to, must not, could –
comparison of adjectives – simple if clauses – past continuous –
tag questions – ask/tell + infinitive …

While I was writing these words in my diary, I decided what to do. I must try to escape. I shall try to get down the wall outside. The window is high above the ground, but I have to try. I shall take some of the gold with me – if I escape, perhaps it will be helpful later. *Dracula*

STAGE 3 • 1000 HEADWORDS

… should, may – present perfect continuous – *used to* – past perfect –
causative – relative clauses – indirect statements …

Of course, it was most important that no one should see
Colin, Mary, or Dickon entering the secret garden. So Colin
gave orders to the gardeners that they must all keep away
from that part of the garden in future. *The Secret Garden*

STAGE 4 • 1400 HEADWORDS

… past perfect continuous – passive (simple forms) –
would conditional clauses – indirect questions –
relatives with *where/when* – gerunds after prepositions/phrases …

I was glad. Now Hyde could not show his face to the world
again. If he did, every honest man in London would be proud
to report him to the police. *Dr Jekyll and Mr Hyde*

STAGE 5 • 1800 HEADWORDS

… future continuous – future perfect –
passive (modals, continuous forms) –
would have conditional clauses – modals + perfect infinitive …

If he had spoken Estella's name, I would have hit him. I was so
angry with him, and so depressed about my future, that I could
not eat the breakfast. Instead I went straight to the old house.
Great Expectations

STAGE 6 • 2500 HEADWORDS

… passive (infinitives, gerunds) – advanced modal meanings –
clauses of concession, condition

When I stepped up to the piano, I was confident. It was as if I
knew that the prodigy side of me really did exist. And when I
started to play, I was so caught up in how lovely I looked that
I didn't worry how I would sound. *The Joy Luck Club*

BOOKWORMS · FACTFILES · STAGE 1
Scotland
STEVE FLINDERS

More than 20 million visitors come to Scotland each year. Some
love it for its long white beaches and quiet green hills. Some like
the busy cities, with their shops and museums, castles and parks.
Others come to see the home of their parents and grandparents, to
hear Scottish music, to find their family tartan. And some come
to visit the whisky distilleries, eat wonderful food, and go to one
of the world's biggest street parties. Scotland has something for
everybody. Come and find what Scotland has for you.

BOOKWORMS · FACTFILES · STAGE 2
Marco Polo and the Silk Road
JANET HARDY-GOULD

For a child in the great city of Venice in the thirteenth century,
there could be nothing better than the stories of sailors. There
were stories of strange animals, wonderful cities, sweet spices,
and terrible wild deserts where a traveller could die. One young
boy listened, waited, and dreamed. Perhaps one day his father and
uncle would return. Perhaps he too could travel with them to great
markets in faraway places. For young Marco Polo, later the greatest
traveller of his time, a dangerous, exciting world was waiting . . .